MW01612647

Now That You're Gone

(The First Year in the Life of a Daughter After the Death of Her Father)

by
Cindy Sanders Crouse

PublishAmerica
Baltimore

© 2005 by Cindy Sanders Crouse.
All rights reserved. No part of this book may be reproduced, stored in a retrieval system or transmitted in any form or by any means without the prior written permission of the publishers, except by a reviewer who may quote brief passages in a review to be printed in a newspaper, magazine or journal.

First printing

At the specific preference of the author, PublishAmerica allowed this work to remain exactly as the author intended, verbatim, without editorial input.

ISBN: 1-4241-0712-1
PUBLISHED BY PUBLISHAMERICA, LLLP
www.publishamerica.com
Baltimore

Printed in the United States of America

Now That You're Gone

(The First Year in the Life of a Daughter After the Death of Her Father)

DEDICATION

I dedicate this book to my Hero, my Father, and my Friend,
Bobby Lee Sanders
Without you, where would I be.

ACKNOWLEDGMENTS

I would like to thank my husband, Charley, who held me through sleepless nights, carried me when I couldn't walk, and wiped my face when it was soaked with tears. You are more than you'll ever know and I love you more!

I would like to thank Garret, Bobby, Britney and Patrick. You all have made me stronger just by watching you.

I would also like to thank my mama, Dale. Watching you has been a pleasure, knowing you has been an inspiration, and loving you has made me strong.

Chapter One

TEACH ME TO BREATHE, LORD

Moment by moment I sat there watching his chest move slowly up and down. The nurse had earlier told me anything slower than ten breaths per minute indicates it will not be long. I counted only nine. I sat there staring at the skeleton of a man with resemblances of my father. It seems like a lifetime ago when those strong leathery hands held a hammer. Now I'm sitting here praying to squeeze a another breath from the body of this man who brought life into mine.

"No one in our family will die from cancer." Daddy said. "It doesn't run in our family."

Many other things did, heart disease was one. In 1982 Daddy had open heart surgery and was given a blood transfusion. Unfortunately it wasn't until much later, ten years later, that we found out the blood was tainted with Hepatitis B. By the time we found out, the hepatitis had turned into cirrhosis of the liver. Daddy was referred to a specialist but the news was grim. He had only six weeks to live. My family immediately started making phone calls and started a prayer chain throughout our community.

"Trust in the Lord with all your heart, lean not own your own understanding..." kept replaying over in my mind. Two months later at a doctor's visit the news was impeccable. His liver was regenerating itself. It was now working fifteen percent rather than the ten percent only two months ago. God had heard and answered our prayers the way we had hoped. The Hepatitis B went into remission and although Daddy still had cirrhosis, enough of his liver regenerated to keep him alive.

"Don't count me out yet." Daddy said.

Ten more years of annual checkups proved to be rejoiceful until this last one. It was August 2002, Daddy had not been feeling well and he was retaining fluid around his stomach. At his annual visit to his liver specialist, Dr. Wade Sutton, blood work was done. Doctor Sutton called a few days later and said the blood work looked fine, but Daddy kept on getting sicker. His stomach continued building fluid and he couldn't eat much. Whatever he did managed to get down, wasn't long until it came back up again. My mother insisted going to another doctor. Blood work and tests were run again but the news was not good. Daddy had cancer of the liver and it was progressive. There was nothing that could be done. He had two to six months to live.

Twenty-three days after the devastating blow I found myself sitting and trying to squeeze out another breath. This time God heard our prayers but decided to answer another way. Daddy died that day. He went home while I was left except for the part of me that he took with him.

My Journal Entries

DAY 2

Why? I don't understand. Why take him? Please take me instead. Why? Why? Why?

DAY 7

I can't stand this! Who are you? You took him! You lied to me! You said you would heal him. Why bring me to Isaiah, just to tease me? Yeah, you really love me. Now what am I suppose to do? No Daddy, no Daddy, no Daddy. How am I suppose to live? I can't and it's your fault! You could have healed him. No Daddy because of you!

DAY 10

How am I suppose to go on. I can't wake up and go on with my day like nothing has happened. I see people doing what they do everyday. STOP! STOP! STOP! I say. Life has changed. Bobby Lee Sanders is not on earth anymore. Everything is different. Quit living like it is not. Quit being happy, quit laughing. I'll never laugh again. I'll never be happy again.

DAY 11

Has this really happen? Did you really take my Daddy? You have made a big mistake. Bring him back now! Don't you see? It's a mistake. You were wrong. You can't take him. What am I going to do? He's my daddy, God. He's my daddy. Why did you do this, Lord? Why?

DAY 17

It doesn't seem like Daddy's been gone for seventeen days. I want to go and dig him up. I wonder what he is doing right now. God, how lucky you are. You have my daddy. Did you listen to me at all when I made all those deals with you? You made deals with Abraham for Lot and gave King Hezekiah fifteen more years. What happened to me? Am I not good enough? It's my fault. I didn't try hard enough did I? Daddy would still be here if I had been better. I'm stupid, stupid, stupid.

DAY 19

Okay, Mister Mighty God, what are you going to do now? You took away my daddy, what's next, my kids, my husband, oh wait, I know, my mama. Let's just make it a combo. Let's take away Cindy's world. Let's see if she can make it without a family. Oh Lord, you're all I need!

DAY 20

God oh God, why did you do this? Why ?

DAY 23

Did you take a break God? Hello, are you there?

DAY 31

He's been gone one month. Where are you Jesus? Please come back. I need my daddy. God, I can't talk to you right now. I now you think you did the best thing. But you did not. You took my rock. The center of me. What do I do now?

DAY 35

I love you God. I love your grace. I know I could not have gotten through these days without you. I'm so glad that you still listen even when I'm fussing. Thank you for not getting mad at me when I'm mad at you. Please tell Daddy I love and miss him.

DAY 45

Oh the pain, God. It will never end. There's no hope in my life. You took that away forty-five days ago. I was Daddy's little girl, now who am I? I'm nobody. You took my life. You touched his body and healed him plenty of times, why not this time? Why not now? Why not bring him back?

DAY 46

NOW

Who knew I would be the one sitting here

trying to find my way through this pain

How did I forget how to breathe

something so simple to learn again.

Words are just empty

my soul depleted

Change not wanted

but it's here

Sour tasting change

go away and bring back

my love.

What good can come of this

Who can benefit

Who can soar

I'm on my knees far from the sky

begging to understand

not really caring

just wanting my love back

Just bring him back to the way

it was before

Leave change

You're not welcomed here.

Reality

At the onset of Daddy's death, the grasp of reality had not set in. The undeniable loss was my only focus. There was no acceptance to be had, only pain. Emotional torment followed me as I replayed over in my mind what I should have done. I blamed myself, feeling if I'd only been a better person, God would have healed him on earth instead of in Heaven.

Closing my eyes at night, I would hear Satan whispering, "You're bad, that's why your daddy's gone. It's all your fault!" So for the first four months, I didn't sleep. While my family was tucked in bed, I would write, watch television, or work crossword puzzles, because when I closed my eyes, it was all my fault and I couldn't stand the fact of letting Daddy down.

No one had ever taught me how to grieve and I didn't understand the flow of emotions that I encounter. I had to keep reminding myself to breathe.

As I sat there and stroked my daddy's face, I secretly was planning to join him soon. Thoughts of being with him within an instant took control of me. No one or no thing took first over this.

Finally one day God got my attention and said to me, "Would you give your own children this same pain?"

"Of course not." I audibly said.

"Then don't think like this again." He added softly.

Through this, good-hearted people came by, called or wrote. But they all had empty words except for the ones who had mourned before. I realized that if you have never experienced the loss of loved one, then you are not qualified to make judgments on the feelings of the ones who have. It is for the best, it was his time, at least he's with God, he's not suffering anymore, are some of the ill-gotten phrases that I remember, hollow words to a broken heart. To those who have never had this pain, simply say, I'm sorry, I'm praying for you, or I'm here. These words will make an impact later in the healing process.

I knew what I felt and I didn't know if I was justified or crazy. God, in my mind, had let me down and I was not going to let Him get by with it. In the preceding journal entries the explicitness was real. I no longer felt God and His protection. I felt alone with no where to go.

God had disappointed me. What I didn't know was that these feelings were normal. The intensity to which I was in pain only signified the amount of love and honor I had for my daddy. My only focus was on my loss not what I had been given—the tremendous love I had been able to share.

Shock

When someone we love dies, we may experience shock, an emotional numbness. Shock is an built-in buffer that helps us accept the devastating news of fearful scenes of death. Philip W. Williams in his book entitled, *When a Loved One Dies,* writes: "God has built into us this natural buffer for the initial blow. It is a good gift because it protects us. There is no way for any of us to totally comprehend the initial loss of a loved person. Shock numbs us and gives us time to get ready for our bereavement journey. We need it, yet only for a time. Then we must move on."

The grieving process certainly will have strong and emotional feelings. Understanding these will help you be able to cope better through this sad and lonely time.

I remember walking around in a daze for days after the funeral. There are still hours I can't account for. Looking back now I see I was being carried all along. Even while I was not acknowledging God, He was still acknowledging me.

Emptiness

The feeling of emptiness, especially if you had a close relationship with the person, is evident. Part of the healthy grieving process is to feel the emptiness and sadness of the 'void' that has been left as we come to accept reality.

Nothing else seemed to matter as my thoughts were continually on my daddy. His presence was no longer with me and although my rational mind knew he was with God and in no more pain, my flesh could think of nothing but the loss I had suffered. My world as I knew was gone. This big space was left and I didn't know what to do. My whole life I had my daddy, now I was suppose to go on and continue to live. What others couldn't see was that I didn't know how.

Everything I knew had just changed. I didn't know how to live without my daddy and I didn't understand why I had to.

Guilt

Feeling guilty over what I should have done or said came next. I remembered back to when I was little and the mistakes I'd made. I thought of how I must have hurt Daddy. Even though I knew it was past, I couldn't keep from dwelling on it.

"If only I had been a better person, God would not have taken him. Maybe I should have fasted before he died." I kept thinking. It seemed God took Daddy to get him away from me because I wasn't a good daughter. I wanted so badly to blame his death on someone that I chose myself as an easy target. I was already down and I couldn't and wouldn't fight back. He would have had a better life if I'd been a better person, I thought.

Fear

I was afraid of what the future would bring. I couldn't stand to think of going on living like nothing had happened. I wanted to shake everyone in my path and shout to them,

" Hey, life is over as I know it!" Seeing people walk around town doing their everyday things was and still is the worst. I see a little blue truck go by and for an instant I think it could be my daddy but then remember. I was afraid of tomorrow. I couldn't even comprehend what I would do.

My husband, Charley, couldn't understand because he had never lost anyone so close to him. I knew I could no longer be truly happy again and although Charley did lose his father-in-law whom he loved, he didn't have the memories and the bond I had shared with this man. Because of this it was hard for him to understand my feelings of total despair.

Anger

Anger took hold of me from the beginning. I directed it all towards God. He had all the power. I couldn't understand why He didn't do things differently. I then became angry at Daddy. It seemed like he had just given up. I reasoned if he had tried harder to live, he could have made it.

The Lord answered with a loving heart and said, "He is tired. He needs to rest."

Whenever I saw an older man I would become angry at him. In my mind if Daddy had to die at seventy years of age then every other man should have to also.

Seeing daughters and their fathers together turned my stomach, "They don't love him as much as I love my daddy." I would think.

Then came the songs, how angry I would get at the radio for playing songs that reminded me of Daddy, "How could they play songs like this?" I would scream. "This is not fair!"

Relief

The feelings of relief were the hardest for me to accept because I couldn't understand why I would feel relief over Daddy dying. God showed me later in the bereavement process that it was okay. I felt relief over not having to worry anymore about Daddy getting hurt or being sick ever again. He was safe and would never hurt anymore. This brought mixed emotions on its own. I could rest now and know that Daddy was also resting. He was in the holiest of hands. I had to let go and just let God be God.

Summary

These feelings will probably never go away but will not stay at the same intensity level as at the beginning of this bereavement journey. Coming to terms with Daddy's death has been a long and weary journey for me, one which I didn't chose to take. God knows what we need when we need it and through this last year I needed Him more than at anytime of my life. He truly at times had to teach me to breathe again.

Chapter Two

WHAT ABOUT ME

My Journal Entries

DAY 52

I can't do this! This is not fair! Why must I suffer? Why did you, the One who is suppose to understand me, why did you do something so horrible? Why?

DAY 54

This is impossible. You did this! You do all of this!!

DAY 55

How can this be. My daddy is gone. How did life change so fast around me? Where are you God? Are you here? Do you even care that you've left me alone here trying to get my Daddy back. You took him, tell me what I can do to get him back, NOW!

DAY 60

Grayness surrounds me. This doesn't seem real. Reality is not here. Why did you go? Why didn't you fight harder? Why did you just let go? God why did you do this? Why did you take my daddy away? There are murders out there God that you could take, why someone known for his goodness and compassion? Why mine? Why take mine? What did I do? It's my fault isn't it God? What did I do to make you take Daddy?

DAY 62

Are you going to take Mama next because of me? Tell me what it is so I can change it Lord please! Don't you know I will? In an instant I will make myself a better person, just bring Daddy back. I want my daddy back. Give him back Lord, give him back to me now! I will change, I promise. I will fast whenever you say, I will go to church every time the door is open. I will change. Enough is enough Lord, please take this away from me. Please take this pain and bring the object of this pain back to me. Why, why, why won't you? Why can't I have my daddy back? Why? Whose your boss? Who do you answer to? I need help and you are not giving it to me. You are sitting up there looking down and laughing at me!

"Let's see how she will get out of this one!" you say. Well God, You can laugh all You want but just help me. I am just an puppet and You are controlling the strings. Please find it within your heart to help me. Blessed be your name Lord. Blessed are your gifts of grace and mercy to us all.

DAY 68

Lonely never felt so alone.

DAY 72

I need to run. I need to hide. I need to find a way. I need to lose myself. How do I hide?

DAY 73

WHO AM I

The light's gone out

I can't find my way home.

I'm alone and scared

down this long and narrow road.

My life as I knew it

is now far less complete

How do I keep walking

when I can't even sleep?

Who am I

Who am I to open up this heart of mine?

Can't you see

that I'm never gonna be the same again?

I lost my friend

I lost my way

Now I'm waiting for this pain to go away.

Oh, Father teach me to breathe.

What is more than an open door

if you don't know how to go inside?

DAY 75

The darkness that is smothering me can go away. I need to be with my daddy! But for the cost of hurting my children, NEVER!

A SPECIAL GRIEF

The death of my daddy broke one of the longest and deepest relationship I have ever had. He brought me into this world and shaped me into the woman that I have become. It was through his nurturing care that I have my fondest memories. I would be a totally different person today had it not been for my daddy then. It is this irreplaceable loss that has made me wondered, what about me?

Not only am I saying good-bye, I'm losing my childhood. I've lost those hands that held me tight when the thunderstorms woke me from sleep. I've lost that bond that a father and daughter have without saying a word. I lost apart of me. It is a special grief that only children who lose their parents can understand. It is a time when the world seems cold and the warmth is gone. The person that took care of you all your life is now resting in God's arms. And yes, there will be times that you will stand back and cry, "But Lord, what about me?"

EVERY DAY

The overwhelming sense of being alone has wondered into my soul. Friends have gone back to work, appointments are scheduled, plans are made and I find myself just staring up into the sky for a glimpse of Heaven. Heaven seems to be more real, now that Daddy is there. God must be happy, now that Daddy's there.

It's hard to understand why we love the way we do if we get hurt in the end. But without love how would we know it? How could we ever feel the warm feeling inside our bones without knowing love first?

God is God and He understands the trials and pain we go through. He went through them also when His son, Jesus, took on our sins on the cross.

In the mist of this sadness, the overwhelming sense of uncertainty rules my thoughts. How am I to go on? How am I suppose to live now? I don't have a daddy anymore. What about me?

These emotions filled me with such an impact that I became nothing but a question. At a time when every thing seemed useless and I seemed not to matter I found something that I had all along. What is it? God's mercy. He gives us more than we deserve. I deserve a death in Hell but He gives me life. I don't know why the trials come the way they do, to strengthen us or enlighten us, but it is for a purpose. It's not all about me and through this second and third month without my daddy I began to realize it.

I had come to believe that I was the important thing here. My feelings would dictate they way God would run things. I couldn't handle Daddy dying, so he wouldn't. I couldn't handle being alone so I wouldn't be. It seemed so simple until God put it into prospective and I learn that it is not all about who I am but who God is.

Max Lucado writes in his newly released book, *It's Not About Me*, "If God exists to please us, then shouldn't we always be pleased? Perhaps our place is not at the center of the universe. God does not exist to make a big deal out of us. We exist to make a big deal out of him. It's not about you. It's not about me. It's all about Him."

It's hard to give all up when I'm at a place in my life that is alien to me. I've never been put in this place before. I never knew any of my grandfathers for they died before I was born. Both my grandmothers past away, the first being twenty years ago and the second only ten, but even though this hurt, they were my grandparents and my mind fixed upon the fact that I wouldn't have them forever. But losing a parent, a daughter losing her daddy, except for the death of a child, I can't imagine a worse pain. God can though. He played the part when Jesus, His Son, died so that we may live. I search my mind for answers on Daddy's death but then I wonder, God knows with more intensity then I, for His Son had no sin, had no guilt or shame. His Son died a more wretched death than others. My daddy went peacefully and with as much dignity as death came bring, but Jesus, had spit on His face, blood pouring from His wounds, and hung on a cross for everyone to mock, not for a punishment for His sin, but for ours. Yes, I can say with upmost certainty that God knows my pain, and it grieves me with every tear that I shed. Had Jesus not gone through this over two thousand years ago, I could have no hope of ever seeing Daddy again. But I do hope and I plan on not letting go, no never letting go when I do see him again, because even though this hurts too much to breathe at times, I still know that it's not about me.

RESCUE

I've determined that I need rescuing. Webster states that to rescue means to free or save from danger, evil, etc… Well, that's me. Would somebody please rescue me?

What is real now? What can I say for certain that is real? It's not time, for that surely fades. What about death? Is death real? I can say, it is not. Death did not hold my daddy in constraints. Jesus carried him home to a place where death is nowhere around. Death can't be real to the one dying but almost too real for the ones left behind.

Prospective, then, is the real key. When your world has fallen and pieces of you are empty the last thing that is thought of is, "Okay let's put things in the right place." Who cares? I didn't and there are times I still don't. But truly, all things need prospective. It helps make sense of senseless things. It takes cruel and unbearable pain and throws it up into the air. Yes, what comes up, must come down but know that with each toss in the air, God touches it and His strength emits from it.

I can be a selfish person. Everyone in my family can attest to that. But it is okay and actually normal to go through this feeling. You need to grieve every part of yourself. Leave nothing un-turned. Go to every depth of yourself and bring it to the surface. Grieve from your deepest being. You have heard the saying, "Let it all out." Do it. Mourn every thought, cry with every memory. Laugh even. Remember with smiles your last vacation together. Remember the funniest joke him/her ever told. Don't forget to scream and kick and throw what you want. Whatever action you have to take to be rescued, do it. Don't lock it inside. Embrace what God has allowed you to feel and don't hold back.

BURDEN

How can I live the rest of my life without Daddy? He was my backdrop for just about everything. I truly did nothing without first asking his opinion. So it is logical for me to think,

"What about me? How am I suppose to go through and not mess up if Daddy is not here to guide me? God, What about me?"

This man's strong opinion and detailed mind kept me straight. God took him home and I'm left trying to put together pieces that I don't even have because most of them are in Heaven. If Heaven is where the heart is I'm homesick.

This burden is too heavy to bear but I'm not ready yet to give it to God. This unnatural feeling has become natural through my grief and it is at least the most constant thing I have in my life right now. I'm keeping it for awhile and I dare anyone to take it from me.

ALONE

Lonely never felt so alone. Time is no more a help than a flood after a drought. One is the opposite of the other but neither are grand. Time just confirms the loss and loneliness proves that silence is not golden. I'm stuck in a place that is foreign to me. I look for answers but find none. No where I look can anyone explain this to me.

The tears I cry bring some comfort to me for they are not alien. I've cried for so long that at times, they are friends, the only ones that can calm me. Somewhere in the back of my head I wonder if God got it wrong. Maybe he meant for it to be as joyous to us as the one who is going home to Heaven. God must've known the pain that this loneliness brings. He must have thought,

"I need to do something about this."

I have so many questions as to why the pain. Why can't it all be joyful? Why does Daddy winning over death and living with God in Heaven have to bring pain to me? What can't I be happy for Daddy? Why can't I rejoice the way I know he is rejoicing now? Why is lonely so alone? Why is it all about me?

Chapter Three

LETTER OF LOVE

My Journal Entries

March 13, 2003

Dear Daddy,

Life without you is hard, strange without no measure. My love for you burst with nowhere to run but back into my heart. Oh, how I wish for one moment of your face, one smell of your skin, one excited burst of laughter from your sweet voice. You were and still are my hero, my strength and even though you are not present on earth, you are in Heaven and I know now you are finally safe. No pain, no worries. You are praising God, hugging Jesus, walking among the saints. How white your robe must be! The sight from your eyes, is seeing things I can only imagine. You made it! But I am here alone with all your memories. I see your things, your clothes, your books, your handwriting, and the emotions are too much too handle. There seems to be a grayness surrounding me. I feel alone. My daddy is gone. But with everything God gives hope to his saints. And yes, I am one and I have hope. A light that is far or near, only God Himself knows when. I no longer fear the unknown of death, because you have lead the way. You made a path for us all. You are the head of us and I guess it is fitting for you to be the first to check it out. I'm coming Daddy, to be with you forever, one day not soon enough. Until then I will still make you proud. I will teach your grandkids your strength and courage. I will not let you down, no not ever. Rest with God. Enjoy your new found freedom to just be. Be surrounded by everlasting love, be tempted no more. Sing songs with David, laugh with Stephen, tell your grandfathers about us. Let them feel your proudness as you remember. One last thing my dear father, I promise to suck it up until the moment that it is my turn, but then I can only dream of the emotions that will pour from me as I see your face standing there welcoming me in to paradise. It is not good-bye Daddy, it is until then.

Forever love,
Cindy

April 22, 2003

We could tell you were a hero

but others already know

or tell about your strength and courage

or how you loved us so.

We could tell about your smile and laugh

or your strong and gentle hands,

26

but everyone already knows

you were a special man!

Happy Birthday, Daddy!

No More Fairytales

The day Daddy died so did my fairytale of God. Whenever anything went wrong it was okay because God would swoop down and move his magic wand and pres-to, things were back as before. I had this sense that nothing would ever go wrong because God was always there. Right? I perceived God as my fairy-godfather who would take all the bad things away. My image of God was a narrow one. I never bothered to understand God's true self until I found myself struggling to reach up from the bottom. I would pray and thank Him for my food or ask for a favor. But I neglected to realize life is real, death is certain, and God is I AM.

The memories are flooding my mind with all too much emotion. It is hard to handle everyday when what I know to be 'everyday' is gone. How can life just pick up and continue with only a day or two of interruption? How can normal ever be normal again?

What is this thing that keeps happening? Death has lost it's victory but the memories cannot be denied. This tribulation, this trial, has become too much to bear. Without knowing that God is there and He understands my pain, how could I go on? I can't see how others who do not know my God personally can make it through times such as these without hope.

Loving Me

There is one thing that has stayed certain through all this pain. Even though I didn't feel it or want to accept it at the time, God never stop loving me. I truly felt rage for this Spirit who calls Himself God. It began to test my faith. I had been brought up in a Christian home and I knew who God was and what knowing Him stood for. But when you have never been put through the fire, how well do you know how you will turn out. This journey for me, has been my 'fire'.

I have felt God's love around at times but then there's the other times that I felt alone. I have found that it was me who had pushed away from God. He had been there holding me from the beginning. And I was smacking Him in the face the whole time.

God's grace is so sufficient for me. He is the one that has given me the courage to go on. Why do I say courage? Losing someone you love takes your strength away, it takes away everything you know to be. Without God whispering to me,

"Cindy, take one step at a time. I'll be here to catch if you fall." I surely would have fallen. There would be no courage to get up each morning. God's love is constant in a world that is constantly changing.

Measurement

I now measure my time in the months of Daddy's death. I can tell exactly how long he's been gone down to the very minute. I measure everything to Daddy's standards. I focus on his life and what it meant to me. If I focus on anything else right now, I think I would explode.

There are days that I see something on TV that I know Daddy would like to watch and for an instant I think I have to call and tell him, then I remember. The awful truth rears it's head and the instant sanity for me again is gone. He's gone and I'm here but so is Jesus. He has always been here. Even though my daddy is not right now, God is. Whose my Daddy? God is, and His love has gotten me through.

Would I ever wish this hurt on anyone? I think my family would agree with me when I answer yes. How heartless can I be? I'm not trying to be heartless, I just know that to hurt this much means I loved this much and I would not want anyone to go through life not loving or having someone to love.

I know that I am blessed to have had my daddy for thirty-four years. I know that I am blessed to have a daddy that loved me and took care of me. I know how blessed I am to hurt this much. With this it makes me think, if a father being sinful loves his child this much, how much more does your Father in heaven love you?? So then, if God loves me, how much do I hurt Him when I sin, disobey or question Him? I have questioned Him numerous times. I even

28

explained to Him that a mistake had been made and that I would like my daddy back right now! But even in the deepest recesses of my mind, God heard me crying out for whatever it was I needed. I couldn't put a name on it because I didn't know. I just knew that I needed something, anything to take the pain away. Although God didn't take it away, He did give me something that I never thought I would feel; He gave me as much peace as I would accept at any given time. How blessed I am to have I AM.

Chapter Four

THE SILENCE WITHIN

My Journal Entries

DAY 123

I had a dream last night about Daddy. I was sitting in a crowd of people upset that he was dead. I looked over and saw him sitting across the row staring at me. He had the prettiest smile I have ever seen. He was so happy he glowed. God are you telling me this is what Daddy is doing? Please tell him it hurts so bad with him being gone. It hurts. I'm mad that he is gone. Mad at everyone. He was so good. Why take him? There are bad people that need to be gone not Daddy. Please God help. Help me please. I want my Daddy back!

DAY 134

Okay Lord, this has gone on too far. This has not been funny. Bring him back now. I want him back! Right now, right in front of me now!

NOW THAT YOU'RE GONE

Why can't I have this? Why can't I just ask for him back here with me? Why does it hurt so much, why so much pain? I could not do this without you God. I couldn't get out of bed in the morning without you telling me to. I have so much love in my heart for this man, my daddy. I feel I didn't have enough time to tell him or show him. But you feel different, don't you Lord? You know his life has been completed so you took him home. Oh, how I wish you hadn't right now! How I wish his arms were around me and he was telling me how much he loved me.

"I love you too sis." I will hear those words over again in my heart forever until I can actually hear them come out of his mouth again.

DAY 136

Time is passing too quickly yet I want to hurry it up. The faster it goes the sooner I'll be with Daddy. How could it be this long without him? 136 days without my daddy. It's not fair, it's not fair, it is not fair Lord! Why? Because it was time. Time to go, too quickly he left. Oh, how I wish I were there with him. Soon enough you say Lord. Not soon enough for me.

DAY 142

UNTITLED

The darkness seems to enshadow me

up and all around

It seems to take up my breath

and envelopes me with no sound

The quiet place I have entered

doesn't seem to fit

All I have planned for me

or the dreams that I have spent.

So I call upon the name of God

and I listen for His voice

That I may know just what to do

in the absence of no noise.

Sacred is the faith

that I put into Him

for He's not only my Savior

but also my best friend.

I will sit and I will listen

for until that very hour

When my precious Lord and Savior

will show His great and mighty power.

Blessed be the name of the LORD!

DAY 146

I lost my friend and my way five months ago. The lights have gone
out and I can't find my way back home. Where is home? Where is it
now? If home is where the heart is then it's in heaven, as it should be.

DAY 149

I'm sitting here all alone waiting for the day to go by. Don't look at me, can't you see that I'm never going to be the same again?

The Silence

Shh…, if you're quite enough you can hear it. It's among the purring cat, the laughter of the kids down the road and Grandma rocking on the front porch. You can hear it as the leaves rustle in the wind and as the sun shines on your face, it is the calm, sweet assurance of silence, the never ending grace of God's love. Mercy abounds here.

It's always been here but I haven't. I've been off looking for answers to questions I'll never find here on earth. I've been so busy trying to make someone explain to me why this has happened that I lost focus on who was getting me through it.

When I finally decided to sit down and listen to God, I felt I had worn out my welcome, but the best thing is, I've only scratched the surface of God's love for me.

The pain I've been going through for so many weeks now have taught me numerous things and I can only imagine how much more I have to learn. I have been broken and I'm tired of yelling and telling everyone so. Now I'm ready to listen.

Through the stillness of my time with my Savior, I've noticed the silence, the stillness of peace that He puts upon me. I look to my near past and I see Him holding me and taking each step with me. I see Him carrying me through Daddy's funeral and being my legs as I walked away from him for the last time here on earth.

Yes, in the silence of His grace I see His love and I picture myself as a child wrapped up in His arms forever pleading for Him to take it all away.

I never thought I would find this peace and be able to walk again but God knew even before my birth that this moment in time would happen for He is All-Knowing.

He silences me with understanding and keeps me on the path that we all dream for. In the quietness of time, I've found more of myself than I thought I was. This silence that He gives me is where the source of my strength admits. You see, He is there, no matter where I am He finds me. It is I who has to silence myself in order to listen.

In my alone time with God is the moments that lift me up and carry me on. I have found I cannot walk through the hallway of my home without the grace that He freely gives me. He is my recharger for each new day and I find it through the silence of our time together. I don't know how He does it, but wherever and whenever I come to Him He's there. Sometimes I worry that He's getting tired of me,

"It's Cindy again! Man I wish she would just listen the first time I tell her something!" Just like a loving father, he wraps me up and gently holds me ever time without anger.

Charles Stanely writes in his book, *The Source of my Strength,*

"As you think about your life and experience as a Christian, where do you stand in all of this? Do you feel as if you've hit bottom and there's no place to look but up? Does the idea of total surrender scare you? Are you like the drowning man who is still trying his best to keep his head above water?"

As I read this it sounded like me. Yes, I'm at rock bottom, yes, totally surrendering scares me, and yes, I'm drowning and I don't know how to swim. Then I thought about my experience as a Christian. Where do I stand in all of this? I stand on a firm foundation although lately I'd been acting like I was on a sandy shore.

It was only when I stop complaining of my plight that I began to feel a sweet nudge. I was afraid to be silent because I didn't want to hear what God had to say. I was searching for answers but wasn't staying around long enough to hear them. To be still and listen, was about surrender and I wasn't ready for that until I made up my mind to be. No one was going to take it from me, not even God.

Yes, silence can be deafening for it's among the ones left standing after God calls a loved one home. It is silence that crept up on us at times when we least expect it. It can be eerie or welcoming, it's up to the one who it envelopes and the chosen path in which they are on. Although I have sat many times on my front porch and listened to the world around, the silence was there and at the end of my day the freshness of the evening breeze drifting was anything but intimidating. But now I find myself on the other end of silence. The left behind route. My daddy has gone home and I'm left here in all this silence.

FREEDOM

In nothing more than mere silence did I find a place of redemption. How silent it must have been when Jesus took his last breath yet how much was heard.

My soul finds it freedom within silence. It no longer heeds the painful words inflicted upon myself because of my sorrow. It dances in His light and finds warmth there. It is letting loose to be and grasping the hope of eternity.

I wish I could turn back time and Daddy was still here. Just because I'm beginning to understand God's plan doesn't help me to accept it completely, but I know it will come in time. Timing is important. I can't recite a few verses and understand. It depends on where I am in my walk with Jesus. Before now, I wasn't ready, but I'm beginning to be. I struggle daily with my loss. It is so hard to bear and bear alone. So I've chosen not to. I've chosen to come before God's throne humble myself and cry. He meets me there with tears also. I know He cries when I do, some times I feel it. When I grieve I'm not alone either, He is beside me. I can't explain this silence better than with one word; Love.

Oh, the wretched soul I'd be, had Christ not died on Calvary. I am the wretch and thank God, He is the forgiver.

MY PLIGHT

Oh the wretched soul I'd be

If Christ not died on Calvary.

To take away all my wrong

And turn within me a new song.

Oh how His love has changeth me

And brought me strength and security.

I will never walk alone

For Christ will carry me toward home.

BEING STILL

Finally allowing myself to sit alone and meditate on God's word was scary. I knew I needed God more deeply than I was allowing Him to be. I felt I was walking alone like a lost child in the woods searching but finding no way out. It seemed that the longer I kept from listening the deeper 'into the woods' I became. Even in the presence of other people I was alone. I felt no one knew the intense emotional pain I had inside me. How could they? I loved my daddy more than anyone had ever loved anybody. Everything was intensified.

Only after giving myself permission to stop, did I see God had been there all along. He had kept me from falling so far that I couldn't find myself again. I learned it was okay to be silent and listen. God talks louder where no one is competing for His attention.

Looking back now, I see that I was the one who walked away from the other ninety-nine sheep. How glad I am that The Shepard came to find me.

Summary

Through this grieving journey I've learned to be still. The power of the mind is forceful but the heart ultimately prevails. I know Daddy is in Heaven. I know now that he is silent no more in his praises. God has given me strength in my stillness and replenished me from within. There is a long journey ahead, one I know will be for the rest of my life, but then it will be over and my journey will be complete. No more sorrow on that wonderful day, for my daddy will be there, walking with Jesus, as they both accompany me to God's throne.

Chapter Five

NO MAGIC WORDS

My Journal Entries

DAY 154

The days seem long, too long to stay awake for. I just want to sleep. When I sleep I dream about you, Daddy. You are with me and I'm okay. I'm safe. But when I awake, reality bites and your still gone. Oh, why are you still gone!

DAY 156

I need my daddy back. Now, Now, Now, Now!!!

DAY 164

Who knows my pain? Who can feel this way. I will not be well again. Oh, how you are gone from me. I think you God for not being gone. Take this cup from me.

DAY 172

I can not believe that Daddy is gone. He was my hero. He knew me better than anyone. How am I suppose to go on without him being here to help me. I am alone in a cruel world. Daddy's little girl, afraid and scared. God help me from myself.

DAY 176

The day will come when I will see you again. I can't wait. Jesus, come back soon, please.

No Magic Words

The follow are letters that were sent to me from people in the different stages of the grieving process. After reading their stories please take the time to pray for these people and their continued faith in Jesus.

Letter one:

I lost my father when I was nine years old. I did not understand what was going on until Daddy never came home. Being little, I was afraid that I might die also. My mother and I became closer after this. My siblings were older and married, so it was just my mother and me at home. I watched her suffer going from day to day without Daddy, but over time I saw a change in her that made me proud. She was a strong woman and became stronger when she had to become father and mother to me. I will never forget her strength as I watched her take in laundry day after day trying to keep food on our table. When she passed away, I thought my life would be over also. I had a family of my own, but knowing that my mother was gone took apart of me that I dare say I will never get back. We became best friends and I had not only lost that but my mother too.

Letter two:

It is hard to breathe. My little girl was taken from me during the middle of the night while my husband and I laid asleep. We heard no sound, nothing. When I awoke the next morning, my life had changed forever. I do not see how a God can do this to a child. I once believed in Him but now I do not know. I hope to find Him again one day, but not now. It is too painful.

Letter three:

My mother died a few weeks ago after a long illness. During her last few weeks of life I could not bring myself to be with her. I felt guilty over this and doubted my love for her. I never pictured myself being this way. She had always been a strong woman and when I saw her laying there on the bed it turned my stomach. Maybe I wasn't a good daughter after all. But I know I loved her. I don't understand this death thing. But I know how real it is.

Letter four:

My father was my best friend. We worked together everyday. When he died, not only did my heart burst with pain, so did my mind. How can I live without him? God has brought me through so much that I instantly turned to Him. At times I was mad at Him for taking my father and I would tell Him so. I knew that I would be alright and that one day I would be with my father again. It just doesn't take away the pain that I'm feeling today. To God be the glory and may His will be forever done.

Letter five:

God's glory shines in all that is done but after the death of my sister it was hard to accept. She was only sixteen when she was in car wreck just one day after Christmas. At first I was in shock and went through the motions with my mother getting her funeral arrangements made. But after a week went by, the emotions started flooded my soul. When you say it is hard to breathe, I totally understand. With each breathe I took it was like a knife cutting me deeper reminding me that I'm alive and she is not. I still struggle with a gracious God and death but I know He's in charge.

Letter six:

My baby is gone and I feel God is responsible. He could have saved her if He wanted. It's hard to believe in a God who does this. I'm not sure if I do. I can't think about nothing but her face as she died and the pain that I felt when she went. Was God there? You say He was. But where? I didn't feel Him.

Letter seven:

God was with me when I watched my father die. I could see peace on his face as he was called Home. I was glad that God had allowed me to be apart of his life and now apart of his death. I've been made stronger by His hand through this bereavement journey and I think Him for not leaving me to go it alone.

Letter eight:

I've never been a religious person, but after the death of my wife I started reading the Bible. She was a Christian and begged me to go to church with her. I always refused and told her that God had nothing that I wanted. She would smile and say, "But he's got me, don't you want me?"

When she found out that she had cancer, never once did she get angry at God. I couldn't understand this because I was furious with Him. She took up for Him when we would get into arguments and now how is He repaying her? Through this whole ordeal she was calm and ready to die. It made me start to think if I would be this ready if it was me. I watched her die with a smile on her beautiful face. If death is so bad then why was she smiling. I'm willing to find this out.

Letter nine:

Ten years ago I lost a dear friend in a accident. I was driving and she was asleep in the passenger side. A tractor-trailer truck driver had fallen asleep at the wheel and hit us head on. Pam didn't have her seatbelt on. She flew out of the window and down an embankment. I was knockout and did not know what had happened until thirty-three days later after I had woken up from a coma. Pam was not a Christian and neither was I. I took a long time to come to terms with her death and knowing that she is in Hell. But God used her death to save me and I will always be grateful to her for that. I still wake up some nights in cold sweats so I start talking to God and ask for His strength. I get it and am able to go back to sleep.

Letter ten:

I know the pain of losing someone you love. My husband died only eight weeks ago. I feel lost and abandoned. At times I am angry at him for leaving me. But most of the time I am grateful to have the time I did with him. We were married for only three years and had not started a family yet. My only memories will be pictures of our time together. My heart aches for this man that was my soul mate. Is he in Heaven? Yes, and I will see he again. God's love has shown through so much during this horrible time. I am certain that God cares for me and wants me to keep on living.

Summary

Hearing the stories of others whose heart have been broken, helps me to understand better about my journey. Reading these letters, especially the ones who still has not 'gotten
it' yet, brings me to my knees.
Each of us are planted here on this earth to help others. I go through this pain so that I can help others who are going through it also. We are God's extended hand. He loves us through other's pain and acceptance.

Chapter Six

WHERE MERCY LIVES

My Journal Entries

DAY 160

I had a dream last night. It seemed so real. You were by my side and we were talking about everyday things. But in my mind I was thinking, "I can't believe you're here. YOU'RE BACK!" Then my alarm went off and woke me up. It was like I had lost you all over again. Too much pain to bear, so I turned off the alarm and forced myself back to sleep. I don't have to think when I'm asleep, so it is the best place I know to go. I wish you were here, Daddy. I miss you so much.

DAY 164

God, why does this have to be my life now? I don't like this new way. I want the only way I've ever known back. Please God. Dear Jesus please help me.

DAY 172

It's so hard to imagine. It's not getting any better. It's so not fair. God bring him back. Just help me. I love you Lord. I know You are the Creator oh, but how I wish you had made a mistake and then brought Daddy back home.

DAY 184

Too much time on my hands. I can't help remembering how Daddy died. God I know you tell me to focus on his life but part of his life was when he died. Will I ever feel normal again? No. I can't Daddy's gone. I need a way through this.

DAY 188

Undeniable pain. Help God.

DAY 204

God I know this went through your hands first and I know You thought I could go through this because it would not have happened if I could not. This makes me mad at myself for being able to.

DAY 215

You are great God. Thank you for being here for me. I know You love me and it is only with Your strength that I have come this far. Thank you.

Promises

God never promised us forever on earth but it is second nature in Heaven. You and I must decide where the end is and prepare for it. Faith will keep us safe along the way. I know no better way to start living without my daddy then by believing that one day I will see him again. It has been my faith in God and his Son that has covered me without blame of the feelings and outpouring indemnitions that I have put upon Him. Mercy lives and I thank Jesus for that. It is a means of transporting myself to the Throne of God and spiritual seeing Daddy worshiping Him.

Mercy takes on many forms, for God can use any and all things. When my sons cry over the temporary loss of their papa, mercy is formed in the hugs from the closet giver. It's not a hard thing to believe and accept as an outward empowering love from the Holy One.

God's Sovereign Will

Romans 9:14-18 states, *What shall we say then? There is no injustice with God, is there? May it never be! For He says to Moses, "I will have mercy, and I will have compassion on whom I have compassion." So then it does not depend on the man who wills or the man who runs, but on God who has mercy. For the Scripture says to Pharaoh, "For this very purpose I raised you up, to demonstrate My power in you, and that My name might be proclaimed throughout the whole earth." So then He has mercy on whom He desires, and He hardens whom He desires.*

That's tough stuff. But only when I truly begin to understand that I was made not to understand did this become understandable. Do you understand? You see, God is God and He can do anything He wishes to do. He even made some of us, such as Pharaoh, for a harden heart just so He could be glorified. Does it seem God is on an ego trip? So what if He is. He's God and He has the right to be on anything He wants to be on. Bottom line is this: God said it, I believe it, that settles it. Hey I'm just glad I'm one of the ones He has chosen to give mercy to. Chances are if your reading this book, you are a blessed one to, for a harden heart would not pick up this book.

God has chosen me to give his mercy to and he has freely given it to me in the last few months. I can't imagine a life without it. Probably because I would have none. I would have just laid down beside my daddy and join him in paradise.

Forgiveness

I was so mad at God, myself and even Daddy. God was first because one whisper from His lips could have changed everything.

44

Why didn't He. Why couldn't He have spared Daddy one more time. Why was this the end? There had been so many near death experiences for Daddy but God had come through and saved the day every time. What was so different about this one? I cannot explain the turmoil when I found out about Daddy's cancer and that it was progressive. He lived only twenty-three days after we found out. Which was a mixed blessing. We didn't want Daddy to die but at least he didn't suffer long. At least he didn't have to wake ever morning for months wondering what the cancer was doing to his body. That's mercy we received. All good mercy.

I had to learn to forgive myself because I thought I should have tried harder to save Daddy. I knew this time was different, even though I could not say it or admit it. I could sense that it was time and I think Daddy knew that to. He had such peace about him. He told me one day about a week before he died,

"Sis, don't get me wrong, I don't want to die but I'm okay with it. If It is my time then it is my time."

That's when I became angry at Daddy, "How could he just give up. This is not fair. Doesn't he know that I am depending on him for the rest of my life. How am I suppose to do this without him. How selfish can one get!"

Little did I realize, it was I who was being selfish. Daddy was tired he had lived seventy-one years and they had been great years. He had been married to Momma for almost forty-seven years and had four kids. He had a good name and was honest. Yes, he knew it was time and truth be told, so did I. But I kept telling myself, what kind of daughter would I be if I just gave up. So I didn't and in the end, I was the one left turning to God saying,

"Lord, I'm sorry."

Chapter Seven

28 THINGS WE MISS MOST ABOUT PAPA

This is a poem my boys wrote after Daddy's death. Out of the mouth of babes...

28 THINGS WE MISS MOST ABOUT PAPA

1. He was a handsome man. (Everyone says I look just like him.)
2. He laughed in a funny way. (I try to laugh the same way but it hurts my throat.)
3. He would always give me money from his shirt pocket. (Sometimes he would have to reach into his wallet and he had BIG money in there.)
4. He let me comb his hair anyway I wanted to. (He looked so funny but he always loved the way I did it.)
5. He would let me go to his body shop and play around in it. (It smelled different but it was how Papa smelled when he came home from work so it was okay.)
6. He would take up for me when Mama was mad at me. (Even

when it was my fault.)

7. He would lay out his teeth on the table beside his chair. (I tried to do this but mine wouldn't come out.)

8. He would hold his bb gun and let me pull the trigger. (Never try this one by yourself.)

9. Nannie would always have to take off his socks while he was sitting in his chair. (He had smelly old feet

10. He would give me lots of candy. (Only when Mama wasn't looking.)

11. He would play card games with me. (He wasn't very good, I always beat him.)

12. He would let me make funny faces with his face. (He looked real scary sometimes, but I wasn't scared, he's my Papa.)

13. He would let me watch football with him. (He would get mad sometimes at the TV.)

14. He would slept, watch TV, read the newspaper, and listen to the radio at the same time. (He always knew when I would try to turn the TV. I still don't understand how.)

15. I miss how he would say my name. (Or call me a name.)

16. He coached softball and never got mad at his team. (The umpires are a different story.)

17. He put three totaled cars together and made one out of it. (It looked brand new.)

18. He would pile car parts around his yard. (Nannie would fuss about this.)

19. He always wore blue jeans. (Except for church and people would tell him, "You clean up well.")

20. He cut off a pair of blue jeans one summer day for shorts. (I've never seen such white legs!)

21. He would always drive slowly. (Sometimes just to make the teenagers behind him get mad.)

22. He always drove little blue trucks. (I never realized this until he died.)

23. He would pick his teeth with a small plastic calender card. (I never used it to look at the date.

24. He would drive in his truck down to the garden in the back yard. (When it had rained his truck would get stuck in the mud and he would get angry but I can't say what he said.

25. He had a tattoo on his arm from the Navy that read, Sandy. (It was his nickname.)

26. He would always keep his head down after I prayed for our food. (He couldn't hear well so he never knew when I said Amen.)

27. He would always sing in church. (Sometimes he messed up the words.)

28. I miss him being my papa. (He still is, he's just in Heaven now.)

Acceptance

It's hard to understand when you're young that death is forever. My youngest, Bobby, which was named after Daddy, was six when Daddy died. Bobby knew that Daddy was in Heaven but he kept asking when Papa was coming back home. I tried to explain to him that Papa was Home and we are waiting until we can be there too. The concept of forever is not conceivable to a child. So the explanation should be on the maturity level the child is.

Garret is my daddy made over. Daddy's childhood pictures look just like Garret does now. I look at my eldest son at times and I see my daddy staring back at me. This brings me comfort and I hold onto this gift that God has given me.

Britney, my oldest, was practically raised by my mom and daddy. I was young when I had her and lived at home with them most of the time. If she hadn't had the influence of Daddy as a child I'm sure her adult life would be different.

It's hard to tell your children that their Papa is gone. It's harder to see their faces as they realize what was said. When the shock wore off and the pain started to set in, it was important for me to be there for them and talk about Daddy and how safe he was now.

My kids love to hear stories of their Papa. Even if they have heard them over and over again. It is important to share the memories of him with them and help them not to dwell on his death, for his death is certain but his life was too. We celebrate him with tears and laughter.

Accepting Daddy is gone is too much to bear at times. Acceptance is a decision and not a feeling, at least up front. The feeling will come later. I can understand that Daddy is gone now and I try to accept it the best I can. At times it is like in the beginning and I have just lost him, but other times, I can laugh at the things he did and smile at this memory.

God has a way of taking my pain and turning it into a lesson that teaches me strength. I never thought I could handle Daddy dying until he did. I took Daddy's hand and told him we would be okay. I told him to let go and go Home. I did this and for me it was a miracle only God could have been behind. He stepped into me in one of the most important scene of my life. He gave me hope when I was staring into Daddy's eyes. He covered me with his mercy as I caressed my daddy's face. God gave me hope and that's all I need to live on.

Chapter Eight

THE POWER OF LOVE

My Journal Entries

DAY 244

I miss you Daddy. Has it been this long? I thought I would never be without you this long. I wish you hadn't died. Oh, how I wish.

DAY 248

It's been so long. I really need to see your face. God let me dream about you. You were looked so happy. I can't wait to be with you again.

DAY 251

This time is shattering. Why Lord? Why?

DAY 257

How can this pain ever end, no it won't. I just have to live with this. Is this my new normal? I guess it is. Pain as normal. Why?

DAY 266

I saw a man today that reminded me that I had lost you. He didn't say a word but for some reason he reminded me of you. I wanted him to be you so badly. You are gone and I am left. Why do I have to be left? Because I have your grandkids to take care of. Jesus come back soon. Please.

TELL ME

What can I do for you Lord

What can I do today

The clock just rang and it's time

to start a brand new day

The first thing I crave from you

I long to hear your voice calling my name

because I need to hear you say

You need to run

You need to fly

You need to tell the people

this is why

One sweet day

I'm coming soon

So this is what I need from you.

Take all the pride from me Lord

and fill me with Your grace

overflow my cup

show me my place

because I need to hear You say

You need to run

You need to fly

You need to tell my people

this is why

One sweet day

I'm coming soon

So this is what I need from you.

TWO SIDES

It doesn't mean a thing

It doesn't have a care

it takes a life and slams it, anywhere.

No matter where it leads you

You're there alone to die

and then it laughs goodbye.

It never says good morning

or good night at night

it takes all the darkness

and chokes out the light

it drives out the hope

and throws in fear to bind

and then it steals your time.

But there's two sides to this story

one of good and of bad.

You fall to your knees

and God will hear

He'll take you in

away from your fear

He'll clean you off

and make you white as snow then you'll know

No longer will sin sting

Jesus Christ is now your King.

His Hand

David Foster in, *The Power To Prevail,* simply stated one of the most profound statements I have heard on a positive bereavement journey. He wrote, " My 'eureka' moment came when I saw, etched into the stone between the two dates, a simple dash. And then it hit me: my father's entire life had been reduced to a dash. People passing by could read his name, when he was born, when he died, but nothing about his life. I wondered if I needed to stand there and say to passersby, "I'm part of his dash! He had me, fought in a war, and did a lot of other things in his dash." Instead of feeling sad that my father had died, my soul flooded with gladness that he had lived. Because my father lived in his dash, I am alive in mine."

I have often wondered the same. When I walk around the cemetery and look at the grave makers, I wonder what type of people does it represent. There are babies to grandparents laying under the ground who are finished. Their lives have been transformed. They are in one of two places. How my hearts grieves for the ones not with my daddy in Heaven.

Then I think, about the hearts that were broken with every stone. How many lives were changed forever when that date after the dash went on. How did they continue? Were they torn into like me? Did they go before God and ask for help? What was their new normal?

So much heartbreak is there. But one day, like a thief in the night, the trumpet will sound and Jesus will appear and all those people who knew him will raise and death will not keep them buried. Their bodies will meet their spirit and join together in the clouds as Jesus calls his saints Home.

God's hand is a powerful thing. It leads me to the places I need to go when I don't know where I'm going, which has been most of the time during this past year. His love has shown his power through simply listening to me when nobody else was around. His love has been undeniable when others looked at me like I was crazy, when I lost it in a crowd. His love has changed me into a forgiving person, in which I had to forgive myself. His hand, His love is there, in the pain in the sorrow, and in the tears. He will lift up the downtrodden and set them up on a hill. He showed me the future by looking into my children's eyes. I have to go on and live 'my dash' so my children will feel the gladness that I feel every time I see that dash on Daddy's grave and know that I'm apart of it.

Time

Is it possible to continue to live the same as you did before the death of you loved one? Yes. Is it probable? No. If you have never lost anyone close to you then you won't understand this until you do. When you lose a loved one, depending on how close you are to them, you will ultimately lose apart of yourself. It is a physical pain that wraps around one and seems to tighten more as the shock settles in. But time can be either your friend or foe. Most of the time it is both. You see, time lets you realize how long it has been since you have seen your loved one. But you also know that with each day that goes by, you are one day closer to being with them in Heaven. I have to force myself to remember the latter. It's hard been rational when all I want to do is scream. And scream, I do at times. It releases the bottled up emotions that I hang onto without knowing it.

Journey

God's has taken this journey with me. He has cried when I cried and held me when I was shivering. He knows my pain. He knows the truth of my mind, when I tell others that I'm okay. God knows me and He knows that I could not have gone through any of this without Him. It hurts way too much to do it alone. Even now when I look back I see how He carried me. I don't remember much of those first few days. I, as well as my family, was in a trance, just to get done what needed to be done. How did we do all the things that we did? It had to come only from the Lord. Our minds were shot. We did not know which end was up. The Lord worked through us to give Daddy the best send off we could. Things seemed to work out like clock work and things were done when we had no idea how they had gotten done. We were heart broken and God knew it. So He took the reins and took control. This journey has been taken with God holding us up and nothing more. This journey has been apart of our lives that we will be bonded to forever. We went through, and are still going through, a journey that has brought us closer. Daddy would be proud. Just as we are proud to say, he is our father.

Chapter Nine

SURRENDER

My Journal Entries

DAY 270

I'm overcome my friend, never ending love, surviving pain once again. Forever were You true, all to see, who could tell it's time to lose me. Surrender, I surrender all else fails, there's nothing else. Lord I'm surrendering to You.

DAY 272

I'm making a conscience decision today. I am giving up my doubts. I'm surrendering to You Lord. Take me where I need to be.

DAY 279

God even though I don't agree with You taking Daddy Home, I will accept that You did. But Lord I really don't like it.

DAY 284

Wow, the pain is so real today. It seems just like at the very beginning. I know there will be times like these. Oh Daddy how I wish to see you. I wish for you to protect me from this. I'm lonely without you. So lonely. It seemed you understood me more than anyone else and I miss that terribly. Soon Daddy soon.

DAY 290

I've given up the endless searching of why God took you, but has it made the pain easier? NO!!! You are gone. I want to reach out to you, ask advice. How I wish this had not have happened.

DAY 299

I love you Daddy! I love you Jesus! One day we'll be together again. One day this pain will go away and never return. How sweet Heaven most be. Paradise forever. You are in Paradise, Daddy. How grateful you must be. One day!

Surrender

I've decided to surrender my thoughts to God. I've come to the conclusion that I can't figure out the 'whys' in Daddy's death. I have to let go and let God be God. I truly can not understand why he took Daddy and I will not know until I get to Heaven, but I do know that it was for Daddy's best interest. I do know that God was protecting him from something.

It makes me realize just how much we miss danger with God's hand overshadowing us. What more could happen to us and to this world if God was not controlling it. What do we all deserve? Hell, an eternity in it.

Who am I to question God.

When Job did he got this, *"Where were*
you when I laid the earth's foundation? Tell me, if you understand.
Who marked off its dimensions? Surely you know!" in Job 38:4-5.

God made us for His glory and He can do whatever He please to us. We're His creation not our own. He molded us into the people we have become. He chose us, we didn't chose Him. He knew NOW even before He sat time into place. My surrendering thoughts came from the realization that I could or go crazy trying. It wasn't a feeling it was a decision to let go. A few months ago if anyone would have told me that I would be doing this I would have smacked them. I was going to find out why God had done this then I was going to make Him change His mind and send Daddy back. A few months ago, God had disappointed me. I was the center of all this, not Him. He had done this to me and I was going to get payback. I screamed at God, for His decision to take Daddy. I question Him and my faith. Is He really real? Have I been a sucker this whole time? Is Darwin correct? This is not a light subject. I had gotten deep into my mess and I was crawling around in it. But in the midst of all the clamor, there was a still small voice saying,

"I've got you. Let it out. Everything will be okay. Just trust me."

In a way I felt okay about losing it because I knew that God would be there at the end. I was brought up to know that God is with me where I go, even in insanity. A pastor once told me that you are the meanest to the one you feel closes to. Why? Because you know they will still be there when you calm down. God promised never to leave me, so I tested Him. He was true to His Word as always. He let me pound on Him and spit on Him and call Him cruel and wrong. He cried with me and moaned with me when nothing else would come out of my mouth. He stood with me during the midst of my pain and whispered my name to me when I felt lost.

Surrendering wasn't easy but it wasn't a hard decision to make. God never let me down and He won't let you down either. He is King and He alone can calm your heart in the storm. Say His name when your in pain and a miracle will happen. I guarantee it. He is listening, He knows your heart and He loves you in spite of yourself.

Choice

It doesn't matter what they say

where they are or where they stay

It doesn't matter what they do

because Dear Lord, I chose You.

No more day, no more night

searching for Your protected Light

The deeds been done, it's now through

because Dear Lord I've chosen You.

Hold on tight this is gonna be a ride

I lost my demons, I'm on God's side

I'll lift my hands, I'll lift my voice

I don't care, Lord You're my choice.

To chose is simply to pick one over another. If you don't stand for something you'll fall for anything. Which rock you chose will either bring down the mountain or keep it stable.

Control

The circumstances around me determined my feelings. I had to relinquish the feelings and give up the control I thought I had but never did. Thank God He was patient with me. It was not easy to give up control over something I thought I had control over. God has it all. We do not. At times we think we do but then we realize it has been

God all along. There are times that I want to take it back. I do not know why because I certainly cannot do it better than God. I have to learn to give up the things that are beyond me. God has my back and He has yours also. He does not put anything out there for you to handle on your own. He promised He will be with you through it all. In *The Message*, Proverbs 27:1 states; *Don't brashly announce what you're going to do tomorrow; you don't know the first thing about tomorrow.*

How can I have control over tomorrow if I don't even know if there is going to be one?

It is not what happens to you that matters. It's what you think about what has happened to you that does. Since a thought is what goes on in your mind and something that you can control, you can chose to entertain these thoughts or let them go. A decision has to be made. Live for tomorrow or live for today, one minute at a time.

Chapter Ten

ONE WISH

My Journal Entries

DAY 301

Today is hard. My mind has been on Daddy ever minute since he's been home with You, God. But today it's been seconds. I cry looking at his pictures. I cry looking and smelling his clothes. He would be so proud of his grandchildren! I hope he is proud of the way I'm raising them. They will never forget their papa. I promise.

DAY 303

Today is rough. We have always put up our Christmas decorations on his day every year. This is hard for me to even think about Christmas much less decorate for it. I know that Daddy would get mad at me for feeling this way. I can hear him say, "Sis, you have to go on for your kids. Those boys need a good Christmas." But how can I think of anything else except that Daddy's not going to be here this year.

DAY 307

I made an appointment with my pastor at church but I called and canceled it. So many times I wish I could talk to someone about the way I feel but when it comes down to it I can't. Living is hard right now. First, Daddy is dead, there is nothing I can do to change it. I can accept it or not. It doesn't matter, he still is gone. Second, I have to go on. I may not like how my life has turned out, being thirty-five and without a daddy, but this is the hand I have been dealt. God gave me this one. I have to live with it. Third, I have to hang on to the fact that I will see Daddy again and live forever with him.

I am sad because I can't hear his voice, see his face, or feel his touch, and I'm sad because he is not going to be here for the holidays. I'm sad because I have to remember my daddy instead of talking to him. I'm sad that it was his time and I didn't get more time. I'm sad that life will never be the same again. I'm sad that apart of me is gone and I won't see it again until I'm Home. I'm glad that nobody had anything bad to say about him. I'm glad that God gave me thirty-four years with him.

DAY 312

God, how am I suppose to make it through life without Daddy? How can I put one foot forward and continue to live. Apart of me is gone. I was Daddy's little girl, now who am I? I still can't seem to grasp the truth to this all. How could Daddy be gone and I'm still here? I never thought you would take him, Lord. I never thought I would be one of the ones who lost their parent. No more smiles from him but in my dreams. There really is death and it's so hard to accept. I don't won't to remember him, I want him! I am just a frighten little girl and I've lost my way.

DAY 315

Who can believe it has been so long since Daddy's been with You, God? I bet it only seems like minutes to him. It hurts so badly to be without him. But I understand that it was his time. I wish you would have bargain with me. I would have done anything to keep him here and healthy. But You know my heart and You know how much I love

Daddy. I wouldn't want to take his peace away from him .My pastor says that Daddy can see us from Heaven. My Momma wants to believe this but thinks Daddy would be sad if he saw the pain we are in. The Bible says that there is no pain in Heaven, but I have to believe that he can see us. I have read many books on the subject and have determined that he can see us but he is filled with the knowledge about the things of the earth. So if Daddy does see us sad, he isn't, because he knows the truth. He knows how God is working things out for us for our good and His glory.

DAY 320

He knows the truth. That sounds so magnificent. I can't imagine my daddy seeing God's face and dancing with Jesus. Does Jesus play cards, God you know how much Daddy loves to play them. That would be a sight to see, Daddy and Jesus playing Rook. It must be so much fun up there.

DAY 323

Christmas is suppose to be about family and sharing your love for them. How can I share my love when half has been torn away. This Christmas is different than all the others. I have always loved this time of year, but this year I don't care. I have to put on a smile for my kids and because Daddy told me to suck it up. That's what I'm doing. This is not a happy time this season.

DAY 327

So this is what it is like not having Daddy here at Christmas. I've never not had my Daddy with me at this time of year. Well it sucks! For over three decades I had my daddy here with me. Daddy opened presents I bought for him, but this year his body is laying in the cold dark ground of some ill-gotten place that can't seemed to keep flowers from being stolen off graves. This year my present to Daddy was a stupid flower. This year we were separated. This year I heard not his voice telling me, "Merry Christmas." This year I had to remember. Remembering sucks. Whether I like it or not, I have no choice. Daddy's not gone just living in another place. One day I'll be living there too. Happy Birthday Jesus!

DAY 331

A POEM

when you left I thought my life was over

it took me by surprise

how could I now go on without you

being by my side

and though time is now fading

you will never leave my heart

every memory keeps you present

and never will depart

so strong I found my hero

honest without compare

I now look around and

your face is nowhere

love cannot explain it

for love's not deep enough

how I fell about you, Daddy

it hurts way too much

DAY 333

WE'LL BE HOME ONE DAY FOR CHRISTMAS TOO

We were all together at this time last Christmas Eve

but not long after this you had to leave.

We are grateful for the peace when God called you home

even though when you left, we were all alone.

To most this day is joyful as to us it used to be

but without you here it's sadness and it's hard for us to breathe.

But knowing that you're with Jesus gives us hope for a better day

That soon our Savior's coming, so know we're on our way.

THE WISH

"One question I need to ask you." is what I heard Him say. "Answer honestly and your answer may even surprise you."

I braced myself for what He would say next. What was this question that the Almighty God could possibly ask me.

As if a calm presence came over me the words formed a sentence, "If I grant you one wish and it was for you to get your daddy back today at this very moment, would you wish it?"

My first reaction, my first thought was, "Of course God, please bring him back to me!" But something stopped me from saying those words. I searched the depths of my being fighting with flesh to give an honest answer. I thought about the last eleven months of my life. All the lessons I'd learned, all the verses I'd memorized, all the prayers I'd prayed, and all the tears I'd cried. An honest answer deserved some time.

I wiped away a tear and answered as honestly as I could, "No, Lord Jesus, I wouldn't want him back now."

I finally understood what God had been teaching me all along. No, I don't want to strip him from the only place where he is safe. How could I take him out of Jesus' arms to satisfy me? That wouldn't be love and I do love Daddy too much to get him back now. How can I change my mind so quickly? It hasn't been quick, it's been painful step by painful step. It wasn't a feeling, it was a decision I had to make. I had to chose to live. I had to put one foot in front of the other everyday. I prayed when I didn't want to, I took breaths when I wanted to die, I opened my eyes daily and sucked up the pain. I just went on.

The shortest verse in the Bible is simply this, *"Jesus wept."* in John 11:35.

Why did Jesus cry so hard that He wept in pain? He was Jesus, He knew He was going to bring Lazarus back from the dead. He knew He would see Lazarus again in just a few minutes. Why did He weep? Because Heaven is paradise and Lazarus had been there for four days and Jesus knew He had to rip him out of Abraham's arms and send him back to earth. Jesus was sad to know that He had to bring this world back into Lazarus sight.

Close your eyes. Think of anything that you want more than anything else on this earth. Feel it, caress it, smell it. Now imagine me taking it away. Now double it, triple it, etc… Get the point? How can Jesus give Lazarus the ultimate gift of paradise then just snap him away from it? He did it to glorify the Father and show His power. But was His heart in it?

I don't have the power to raise the dead, but God's question to me raised the awareness of my prayers. Yes, I want Daddy back here with me. But I love him so much that I will wait to be with him when it is my turn to die.

Jesus wept and so does Cindy.

POWER TO PREVAIL

Grief is a common unmistakable sense that consumes even the smallest of us. No one is exempt from what this word embodies. Its very essence brings shutters to the body, for everyone who knows well what this word is, knows that once it's apart of your world, it is always there. Like an unwanted guest that never leaves.

I lost my Daddy to cancer. As much as it is hard to accept, my daddy is no longer beside me. Going through this bereavement process has changed me. I no longer will be the person I was before his death. Apart of me went with him so I'm left here broken.

There's no medicine for this except hope. The Lord my God, gives this to me daily. I have to hope for something more. I've sat on my porch during many 'midnight hours' of my bereavement and think about my daddy's life. His body is in the ground. It is the picture in my mind and memory of my heart that I think of when I think of him. But that wasn't truly who he was or is. His spirit, the one thing that flew away that cold January day was more than his dark brown hair. His soul was that of a great man. He loved his family and took pride in us all. He was forgiving and didn't hold a grudge(at least not for long). He had his own opinion and was usually right. He was a country spirit who loved the outdoors and dogs. He was a honest and stubborn man and all this made him my daddy. This part is what still lives on. He is that spirit that made that body who it was. Being be his side when he died, I felt his spirit leave. Knowing that Daddy went to God, is my comfort. I had the privilege of helping him to the other side, a side where I so badly wanted to go too. I saw the smile on a worn out face and I held the arms that raised to Heaven. I saw, even if it was just for a second, Heaven through my daddy's eyes.

Theologian A.A. Hodge wrote: *Heaven, as the eternal home of the divine Man and of all the redeemed members of the human race, must necessarily be thoroughly human in it's structure, conditions, and activities. Its joys and its occupations must all be rational, moral, emotional, voluntary, and acute. There must be the exercise of all faculties, the gratification of all tastes, the development of all talent capacities, the realization of all ideas. The reason, the intellectual curiosity, the imagination, the aesthetic instincts, the holy affections, the social affinities, the inexhaustible resources of strength and power native to the human soul, must all find in heaven exercise and satisfaction.*

Heaven is home. It has been designed by a loving Savior as a place where we will live together for eternity. Now I know why the Psalmist wrote, "Precious in the sight of the Lord is the death of his saints."
(Ps.116:15)

This world is not my home, so the one wish I have now is this; Jesus, please come back soon!

PRIDE

It has almost been a year since Daddy went Home and I still see the bond that we shared through life still here through death. I am proud to know that one day we will spend eternity together.

My daddy was never one to praise God out loud, but one day I'm going to see him dancing. I'm going be there because my faith tells me so. God is more to me than just my Creator, He is Jesus, my Savior and that tells me I'm there. I won't have to wish anymore, for where I am, He is also.

Someone once said to me, "Having no hope is a scary thing.

Imagine a life without hope. Jesus commands us to, *"Pick up your cross daily and follow me."*

Without hope of something at the end of days why would you go on. I have hope more now then in all my years combined, I have to. I couldn't answer no to God's question without it. In order to go on I must go in hopes of a future with a promise, a destination at the end of life, the pot of gold at the end of the rainbow.

More than not I stumble but God picks me up and helps me to remember the prize, an eternity with Him and Daddy. What a pick me up that is!

Chapter Eleven

IT IS NOT GOOD-BYE, BUT UNTIL THEN

Dear Daddy,

Today is the day I never thought I'd reach. You have been gone for one year. I remember us sitting on the couch talking about the day you would die and how calm you were. I didn't understand it then but now I do, because today Daddy, I am calm also.

Apart of me wants to scream at this but another parts knows why. You are safe and you know to the extreme how much I love you. You are among the saints happy and secure.

It is hard being down here and living without you. I see your face in my boys and hear your laugh in theirs. I know I have to grow up now but I'm still your little girl. I must find my place in this world without you, how sad I am that I have to do this. There are still times when it is hard to comprehend that you are gone. Oh, how can I?

You were and still are a great Dad. I am very proud to have your features and blood running through my veins. I will always try to make you proud. Daddy, I will go on and live. I miss you with all my heart. It is still hard to breath at times and the pain of losing you so soon is present daily. I will suck it up and be a wife, mother, and one day, grandmother too. I will love my family, friends, and enemies, just the way you taught me. Your memories will always be upon my mind and your name will be a constant. Make room for me Daddy, for one day, I'll be there. I can't wait to see you again. I can't wait to see what you have been doing since you've been there.

I hope you found somebody to cut your hair the way you like it, not taking too much off the front. I know it's great to see out of both eyes again and not have to walk with a limp anymore. I wonder, is your tattoo still there or did God take it away? Tell Granny I love her. We'll be fine, don't worry, God's got our backs. One last thing Daddy, thank you for sharing the mashed potatoes, shaving off your mustache, working so hard, the cars, the money and the good times. I love you and remember one thing more, Daddy, this is not good-bye, but until then.

With forever love,
Cindy

I don't like the fact that my Daddy's gone. In fact, I hate it. The good thing is, it's okay. God understand this. He knows the rollercoaster of feelings that I have gone through this past year. I know I will make it. I've come to realize many things about God and myself during his journey. I know that Daddy died. I either can accept this and go on or do not accept it. It will not change the fact that Daddy is gone. A Christian counselor once told me my kids would one day look back and say,

"When Papaw died our whole world fell about." or

"I miss Papaw he had the funniest laugh." It was up to me. It was a conscience decision I had to make. Daddy's gone but I'm still here. Everyday I have to remind myself to put one foot in front of the other. It's easier now and I'm learning. Everyday I think about him, I even ask God to tell him things for me. I can't imagine why God wouldn't. Life has gone on with me here on earth and with Daddy in heaven. How I wish I were there but not until my time.

I've read many books on the subject of Heaven since Daddy's been living there. It makes me feel closer to him.

70

All have said the same; there is no break in conscienceless and all his memories are restored with greater clarity. He knows now. He knows why things happened the way they did. He knows why he died when he did. He's singing now and dancing with greater joy. My Daddy is praising God in a way I've never known. He's living to his potential and wanting me to live to mine.

I must warn you that those who are in heaven cannot communicate with us. The Bible strictly forbids any attempt to communicate with those who have died. We must realize that they are more knowledgeable than we and someday we will be with them. I have learned to entrust Daddy into God's care.

This is the hardest place I've ever been in, but the peace I feel is amazing. The flesh side of me still calls out in anger to God but my soul knows, it knows no boundary of the love I share with my Daddy, and dying doesn't just erase it. I miss his face, I miss his jokes and I miss his touch, but we are not separated for forever.

"In My Father's house are many dwelling places; if it were not so, I would have told you; for I go to prepare a place for you. And if I go and prepare a place for you, I will come again, and receive you unto Myself; that where I am, there you may be also. (John 14:2-3)

I cling to this promise for one day I know that I will see Daddy again. Jesus says so, and I believe it. The separation that God has given us is for a reason. I don't know why and I wish it could have been different, but Daddy's home and that's the way God needed it to be. He probably needed a coach for His ball team or somebody to fix up his pickup truck and He needed the best so who else would he chose. My daddy is a real daddy. He loves us with all his heart and even if he cannot see us I'm sure he ask God quite often how we are doing. Death does not stop love it just empowers it. I've found out through this ever so long year the depth of my love for my daddy. I know that love is real and it is given by God for us to enjoy and experience life more fully. No one can truly live without the power that love gives us, the cold rainy nights when we're all alone is not so lonely when the memories of love are there. The passion that stems for the conditions of love multiply in bounds every day without boundaries. Heaven is like that I believe. The very presence of God is love, oh how Daddy must feel surrounded by the maker of us all!

I still feel Daddy's presence around me and I know he's here. I'm sure he still gets upset at me when I do wrong for he knows the consequences. Just like always he's watching over me.

How can I just let go? I'm not. I'm letting God. I've learned I'm not the one in control. I can't do anything unless God allows me.

This side of eternity has it struggles and frustrations, the silence within at times brings no magic words, but when we find where mercy lives the power of love will help us surrender to the one wish we all ultimately have—an eternity in heaven.

The One Year Obituary

An exceptional man of character died one year ago today, January 11, 2003 at his home in Shelbyville, Tennessee. He was surrounded by his family as the good Lord took him home.

He was the husband of Dale Haynes Sanders and the father of four, Joan, Gina, Bubba, and Cindy and had 10 grandchildren.

He was a hardworking man who always had a smile on his face. Everyone respected him even those he didn't like. He spoke his mind and told it like it was. Yes, his hands were calloused and his skin leathery but that was from the countless hours spent doing his greatest passion-body work. He was spoken in every home along with the word-softball-for he loved the game and devoted his life around coaching team after team. He was the Property Assessor of Bedford County for twenty years and retired after he decided it was time. He was known for being the only politician who could run on his name alone.

Wealth is not known for money but for the tears of the ones left behind. As for this man, he was wealthy beyond measure. His loved ones are devastated by his loss and have only the hope of our Lord Jesus Christ that one day they will be together with him again. God bless the Sanders family as apart of them will, for at least a little while, be separated by His will.

Summary

The bereavement journey was new to me but now fits like an old worn out glove. I've grown to become a more passionate person taking nothing for granted.

I live that's all there is to it. God is in control and I have to give it to Him. I can't do whatever I want, I know he gave us free will, but being a Christian, makes me want to do what God wants. I don't have to like it but I must do it, for my sanity, because apart from God I have nothing. I don't see how people without God can live. How can anyone without God's love go through a bereavement journey and come out okay.

The world looks at Christians as fools, believing in something we can not see, but being a Christian, we look at the world and ourselves as sinners but with one thing different, we are forgiven, and that makes all the difference.

Sometimes it's hard to understand that eternity is forever. Our minds are so small that we can't comprehend forever. God made it this way. I don't have all the answers I just have God. So to all the ones that have gone on before us, have fun up there and know, it is not goodbye but until then, til we can be with you again.

Printed in the United States
42556LVS00007B/103-150